Bible references used:
MATTHEW 11:16, 17; 18:1-4; 19:13-15;
MARK 9:36, 37; 10:16; LUKE 18:15, 16

Jesus liked children. One day he was working in the carpenter shop. He looked out of the window. Some children were playing. He stopped his work and stood at the door and watched. He smiled. The children smiled. They knew Jesus liked them.

Jesus wanted children to be happy.
He wanted people to be good to them.
He was glad when he saw mothers and
fathers taking good care of children.

One day, Jesus heard some children singing. They were making music on a little flute. They were singing and dancing to the music. Jesus listened. He liked to hear the children's music.

Another day Jesus was talking with some big people. He was telling them about God. A little boy was there.

Jesus saw him. He called, "Come, little boy. Come near to me." And the little boy came to Jesus.

The little boy knew Jesus liked him. He was not afraid. Jesus put his arm around the little boy. Jesus told the people, "This little boy knows

that God loves him. And he loves God.
You will all be happier if you love God
and trust him as this little boy does."

Another time Jesus and his friends were traveling. A big crowd of people followed them. Jesus' friends were pleased. They wanted a big crowd to hear Jesus.

In the town some children heard that Jesus was coming that way. They wanted to see Jesus.

They wanted to talk with Jesus.
They asked their mothers, "Will
you take us to see Jesus?"

The mothers smiled. They knew their children wanted to see Jesus. They wanted to see Jesus, too.

They said, "Yes, we will take you to see Jesus." And they started along the road.

The mothers and the children
walked and walked. Then they saw the
crowd of people. A little boy called,

"There, look! There are the people.
That is where Jesus is. Let's hurry!"

The mothers and the children came to the edge of the crowd. "How can Jesus see us?" a little girl asked. "There are so many big people."

One of the mothers said, "I see one
of the friends of Jesus. I will ask him to
help us get through the crowd."

The mother spoke to the friend of
Jesus. But he was not glad that the
children had come.

"Don't you see that Jesus is busy? Important people are here. Take the children back home."